SECOND EDITION

Stop and Think Workbook
Second Edition

Philip C. Kendall, Ph.D., ABPP
Department of Psychology
Weiss Hall
Temple University
Philadelphia, PA 19122

STOP AND THINK WORKBOOK
Second Edition

Copyright © 1992
by Workbook Publishing

ISBN: 1-888805-03-X

This edition benefitted from the input many colleagues. A special thanks to Lauren Braswell, Ph.D., James Poling, Ph.D., James Epps, Ph.D., Bonnie Howard, Ph.D., Martha Kane, Ph.D., Kevin Ronan, Ph.D., and Lynne Siqueland, Ph.D. The input of the many youth who have participated in the program is also very much appreciated.

Printed in the Unites States of America
9 8 7 6 5 4

Workbook Publishing
P.O. Box 67
Ardmore, PA 19003-0067 USA
www.@workbookpublishing.com

This <u>Stop and Think Workbook</u> is yours!

Put your name, address, and phone number
in the spaces below.

NAME   _____

ADDRESS   _____

             _____

             _____

PHONE #   _____

TABLE OF CONTENTS

continued on next page...

Table of Contents continued...

SESSION 1: GETTING STARTED

Hi! My name is Detective Dan. Along with your therapist, I'll be working with you for the next several months. Each time we get together we'll be working on several different tasks. This book may look like a lot to finish, but we **don't** have to rush to get it all done. We're going to try and go very slowly and do a good job, even if we only finish a few tasks during each of our meetings.

When we do the tasks in your workbook, we're going to <u>think out loud</u>, and say several things, or steps, as we work. More about this in a minute.

In the back of your workbook you'll find two sheets (the green pages) that contain several **Stop and Think Dollars**. You'll be cutting these out a little later. At the start of each session you get 20 Stop and Think Dollars--they are yours to use to spend on great prizes. On page 111 you will find a **Reward Shop**--and you and your therapist will arrange for prizes for you to earn.

In this workbook each Stop and Think dollar is called a "point." If you do great work, you get to keep the points. But, you could also lose Stop and Think dollars, or points, if you're not careful. There are three ways to lose a point. You could loose a point:

1. <u>If you go too fast</u>. When working in this workbook we go slowly and carefully. If you go too fast, you can lose one point. Remember, it pays to take your time. Don't hurry.

2. <u>If you forget to say a step</u>. We will be saying several steps to solve each task. If you say the steps, terrific, you can keep the points. However, if you don't say the steps, you can lose a point.

3. <u>If you say the wrong answer</u>. The third way to lose a point is easy to understand. If you get the wrong answer to a task or problem, you lose a point.

OK, there's a lot to know--but let's see if we can restate the basic rules. Try to answer the first set of questions. Take your time, and work together with your therapist.

Stop and Think Dollars are also called points. (Circle the correct answer)   YES   NO

How many points do you begin with?   _____

What are the three ways you could lose a point? The first one is provided--you list the others.

1. <u>Going too fast</u>   __

OK, now you try the rest:

2. _____

3. _____

Talk with your therapist, or look back if you need to. Remember to take your time. When you take your time and don't rush you can do a terrific job.

Don't worry, you probably won't lose all or even most of your points. We'll take our time and go slowly, so at the end of each meeting you'll have some points left for buying a prize. Each of the prizes will cost different amounts of points.

Here's a bonus. There are also 2 ways to <u>gain</u> points to add to your total-- we'll discuss them at our next session.

There's one rule about prizes. Each time that we meet you'll have some points remaining at the end. These points can't be spent all at one time. You can spend some points to buy one prize, but you <u>must</u> put any extra points in your bank (page 113), where you can save them up for a bigger prize on another day. For example, if you have 20 points to begin with and lose 5 points, you'll have 15 points left at the end of the session. You can buy a small prize with a few points and put the rest of your points in the bank, or you can put all of the points in the bank. Saving or "banking" your points will help you to earn a bigger prize later!

2

THE STEPS

Remember that earlier we mentioned about how we will think out loud and use "steps" to solve the problems in this book ? We will say these steps out loud each time that we do a task or problem. At first it may be tough to remember them all, but we will practice over and over--soon you will be able to say them as easily as your name.

OK, let's try to learn the steps. You won't know them all the first time you hear them. We don't expect you to. We'll go over them many times.

The first step we'll say is: **"What am I supposed to do?"** We say that so we can be sure we are doing the right problem in the right way. Another way you might say this is "What's the problem?"

The second step to say is: **"Look at all the possibilities."** That means be sure to look at all the different answers so we can find the best possible one. Another way to be sure to look at all the choices is to say to yourself **"Focus in."** That way we remind ourselves to concentrate or think hard about just the problem we are working on right now. We don't need to think about anything else.

The third step is to: **"Pick an answer"** after studying the different choices or possibilities.

The next step is to: **"Check out your answer"**

And, finally, if you had the correct answer tell yourself, "I did a good job!" If the answer was wrong, we don't want to get upset, give up, have to put ourselves down. Instead, we will remind ourselves to "Be more careful or go more slowly next time".

Let's summarize the steps on the next page. Ready? Oh yes, I almost forgot. You don't have to say the exact same words--you can put the ideas into your own words. Talk with your therapist and, in your own words, summarize the steps that you will be saying as we go through your workbook.

1. _____

2. _____

3. _____

4. _____

5. _____

Just for starters, try the tasks that you find on
this and the next few pages and use the steps. Try
to figure out "Which one comes next?" You may know
an answer quickly, but don't jump ahead. Instead,
be sure to say the steps and to go slowly.
Remember, you can lose points, so take your time.
Good luck.

WHICH ONE COMES NEXT?

A   B   C   _____   G   D   E   F

Let's see, the first step is "What's the problem?"
Well, the problem is to find the letter that comes
next in the series. The next step is to "Look at
the choices", and I see that there's G D E and F.
I say A, B, C, and D comes next. I pick D as the
answer. And, since D is the correct answer I say "I
did a good job."

You and your therapist work on the next ones. Think
out loud using the steps. Take turns.

D   E   F   _____   G   D   E   F

M   N   O   _____   Q   R   P   S

A   C   E   _____   G   H   D   F

Q   S   U   _____   V   W   Y   T

1   2   3   _____   5   3   4   6

D   G   J   _____   M   N   K   L

1   3   5   _____   6   7   8   4

4

T U V ____	W X Y Z
7 8 9 ____	14 8 9 10
1 4 7 ____	11 8 9 10
9 8 7 ____	8 6 5 3
9 7 5 ____	2 6 5 3
2 4 3 ____	7 5 6 4
16 8 4 ____	5 1 3 2
2 8 3 ____	2 1 4 9
6 12 18 ____	19 7 13 24
Z Y X ____	W V U T
P O N ____	Q M L K
H F D ____	E C A B
M K I ____	G F N J
C D E ____	G F N J
0 6 12 18 ____	19 7 13 24
2 4 3 ____	7 4 9 10
3 33 2 22 ____	1 22 11 23
2 8 3 9 ____	2 1 4 6

There will be tasks of many levels of difficulty. Some of the questions may be too difficult for you-- That's OK. Work with your therapist to pick the level of difficulty that is just right for you. To help you and your therapist pick tasks that are right for you, the questions have been organized with the easier questions coming first and the more difficult ones coming at the end of the session. If the tasks in any one session don't match your needs, you can arrange with your therapist to bring in some of your schoolwork, or other tasks that are of interest to you.

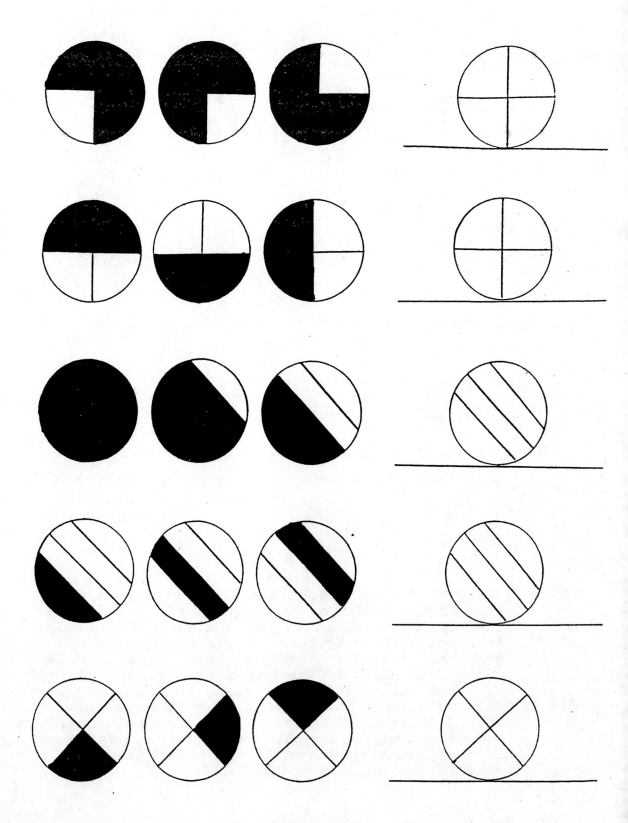

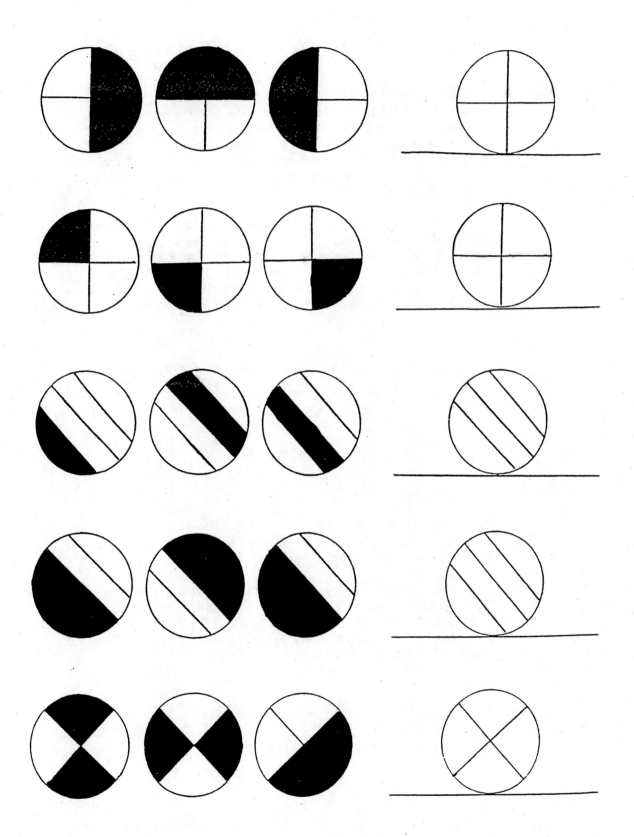

ABOUT YOUR WORKBOOK

In the back of this book you'll find several things to help you with some of the tasks to come. You'll find a large stop sign. We'll use the stop sign as a reminder to Stop and Think. On the back of the stop sign there is a place for you to list the steps--in your own words. When working on the tasks in this book, or when things are going too fast for you, you can pull out the stop sign so you can slow down. If you forget any of the steps use your stop sign to guide you!

You'll also find a pretend magnifying glass at the back of this book. You'll use this later on to help you <u>focus in</u> when we do some word search games. Also there are the Stop and Think dollars (point cards), and some situation cards. You'll need the point cards soon, the situation cards are for later.

Take some time now to cut out the items we just talked about. Keep them handy, we'll use them throughout the workbook.

Finished? Are they cut out? Take the stop sign and turn it over. There's a place for you and your therapist to list the steps. Take the steps that you wrote in your own words and write them on the back of the stop sign.

Great work.

FOR NEXT TIME:

A "STIC" task is something you do to "__Show That I Can__ (STIC)." Each session will end with a STIC task for you, and each new session will start with a review of the previous STIC task. Remember, you want to "Show That I Can."

Here's your first STIC task.

1. Remember the name of your therapist.
To help you remember, write the name here.

_____   _____

If you can do your STIC task for next time you can earn 2 extra points, so try to remember!

Now, let's use the BANK to save your points. After each session you'll have some BANK TIME.

BANK TIME!

Your therapist can give you up to 20 points for your efforts today. You can now spend/save your points.

Total for today _____

Cost of a prize, if you picked one   - _____

Total left to put into the bank _____

Go now to page 113. BE SURE TO RECORD YOUR TOTAL IN THE BANK. Save up your points--you'll be able to use them at a later time.

SESSION 2: FOLLOWING DIRECTIONS

Remember last meeting we mentioned that there are ways of losing points. Recall also that we mentioned that there would be ways for you to earn extra points.

One way to earn points is the STIC task. At the end of last session there was a "Show That I Can" (STIC) task for you to do. At the start of each session you can tell your therapist what you did and you can earn an additional two points. There is a STIC task for each session. We'll do exactly this in just a minute.

Another way to earn extra points is with the "How did I do today" rating sheets that are at the end of each session in this book. Look at the end of this session and you'll see one. After you've done your work for a session, both you and your therapist will complete the "How did I do today?" sheet. You will do this separately. If your and your therapist's rating are within one point of each other you earn another 2 points! That is, you can earn points for being a good judge of how well you did. On a good day, or a bad one, you can earn the extra points by being a careful rater of your behavior.

Before we start, we review the STIC tasks from last week. Remember? Let's do the STIC task now. Did you remember your therapist's name?

1. My therapist's name is_____

If you were able to remember, then you earned your STIC task points. Turn ahead to today's bank at the end of this session and record your STIC task earnings.

THIS WEEK'S SESSION

This week we'll be working on activities that involve following directions. A big part of being able to understand and follow directions has to do with taking your time and not rushing. Remember to <u>Stop and Think</u> before you do something!

Before we begin today, locate your stop sign. Take a minute to read over the steps you wrote on it. As we work on following directions you can use your stop sign at different times and practice using the steps.

You and your therapist will take turns doing these tasks today. Listen, you'll hear the steps being used as your therapist tries to solve the problems.

For your set of tasks today, you will get to read the directions yourself, use the steps, and then answer some questions. Use the steps to do each task. For the first few, you can read and repeat the steps aloud as you do the problems. Remember, each time you rush or forget to use the steps you can lose a point...so take your time! <u>STOP AND THINK</u>. We <u>don't</u> have to finish all the tasks. As you go through the tasks they get more difficult. Almost no one does all of them. Let's take our time and do a good job. Now let's begin...

1. Put a circle around the X.

      C V B T X D H U R T G

2. Put a circle around all of the "R"s.

      E T R Y H F R G M F R

3. If the letter is a vowel, put an X on it.

      Z D A S C E Y H U I O

4. If the shape is a circle, put an X in it.

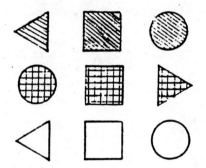

5. If the shape is not a triangle, put an X in it.

6. Cross out everything that is not a circle. Now, put a happy face on the shape that is left over.

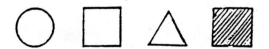

7. Cross out everything that is not a triangle. Now, draw a circle in the shapes that are not crossed out.

8. If the shape is a square, cross it out if it has diagonal stripes.

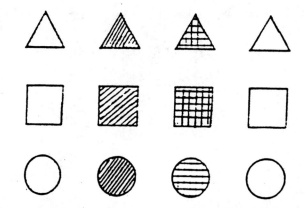

9. Draw a triangle. Put a circle inside it so that the sides of the circle touch the sides of the triangle.

10. Draw a triangle. Put it inside a circle so that the points of the triangle touch the sides of the circle.

11. Help Detective Dan find the Stop and Think sign. Mark the path for him. Be careful...look ahead before you mark the paper. Use your steps to guide you.

12.

Centertown					

O   Arthur Ave.

☐   ☐   ☐   ☐   ☐

Bobby Ave.

☐   ☐   ☐   ☐   ☐

Charlie Ave.   X

☐   ☐   ☐   ☐   ☐

Dave Ave.

1st St.	2nd St.	3rd St.	4th St.	5th St.	6th St.

```
        N
        |
W ------+------ E
        |
        S
```

Use dots (...) to draw a path from Point O to Point X.
Now describe the path.

First I went _____ blocks _____ (direction)

Then I went _____ blocks _____ (direction)

16

13.

```
+------------------------------------------------------------+
|                        Your Town                           |
+------------------------------------------------------------+
|              Annapolis Ave.                        X       |
|     [  ]      [  ]      [  ]      [  ]      [  ]            |
|  O           Boston Ave.                                   |
|     [  ]      [  ]      [  ]      [  ]      [  ]            |
|            Connecticut Ave.                                |
|     [  ]      [  ]      [  ]      [  ]      [  ]            |
|              Delaware Ave.                                 |
+------------------------------------------------------------+
   1st       2nd       3rd       4th       5th       6th
   St.       St.       St.       St.       St.       St.
```

```
                    N
                    |
         W ---------+--------- E
                    |
                    S
```

Use dots (...) to draw a path from Point O to Point X.
Now describe the path.

First I went _____blocks _____(direction)

Then I went_____blocks _____(direction)

14.

```
┌─────────────────────────────────────────────────────┐
│                     Square City                       │
├─────────────────────────────────────────────────────┤
│                                                       │
│      A           Annie Ave.                    X      │
│    ┌───┐  ┌───┐  ┌───┐  ┌───┐  ┌───┐                 │
│    │   │  │   │  │   │  │   │  │   │                 │
│    └───┘  └───┘  └───┘  └───┘  └───┘                 │
│                 Barbara Ave.                          │
│    ┌───┐  ┌───┐  ┌───┐  ┌───┐  ┌───┐                 │
│    │   │  │   │  │   │  │   │  │   │                 │
│    └───┘  └───┘  └───┘  └───┘  └───┘                 │
│      O          Charlotte  Ave.                       │
│    ┌───┐  ┌───┐  ┌───┐  ┌───┐  ┌───┐                 │
│    │   │  │   │  │   │  │   │  │   │                 │
│    └───┘  └───┘  └───┘  └───┘  └───┘                 │
│                 Darlene Ave.                    B     │
└─────────────────────────────────────────────────────┘
```

| 1st | 2nd | 3rd | 4th | 5th | 6th |
| St. | St. | St. | St. | St. | St. |

```
              N
              │
              │
     W ───────┼──·──── E
              │
              │
              S
```

Use dots (...) to draw a path from Point A to Point B.
Now describe the path.

First I went _____blocks _____(direction)

Then I went_____blocks _____(direction)

Hi again! It's good to see that you got this far. Remember to pat yourself on the back and tell yourself, "Good Job!"

Pretty soon, you'll be doing something a little different. That is, after you've shown your therapist that you know the steps extremely well, you can begin to whisper the steps as you do them. That way, you won't bother other people if you were to say the steps out loud.

15. Draw 2 circles side by side so that they touch.

16. Draw 2 circles one on top of the other so that they do not touch.

17. Draw a circle, and then put another one inside of it.

18. Draw a square, and put a circle inside it. Now, put a triangle inside the circle.

19. Draw two squares so that they touch on one side. In the left square, put a triangle. In the right square, put 2 triangles.

Now we can try some questions that have to do with words. Read each word on the same line. Write another word that is the same kind of word as the first three. If these are too easy or too difficult, your therapist can create some that are more appropriate for you.

20. banana   apple   pear   _____

21. blue   yellow   orange   _____

22. bike   car   boat   _____

23. dish   chair   lamp   _____

24. coin   dollar   check   _____

25. Think back to the five tasks above. What were you told to do? Circle the letter of the correct answer.

   a) Think of words that are not the same kind

   b) Think of words that are the same kind

   c) Think of words either the same kind or not the same kind

26. How were you told to answer? Circle the letter of the correct answer.

   a) Say your answer out loud

   b) Write your answer

   c) Just think of an answer

27. Ask your therapist if your answers are correct. If they are correct <u>Good Job</u>! If you have an incorrect answer, go back and try again--you can do it! Go ahead and pat yourself on the back. You're working really hard.

28.

```
┌─────────────────────────────────────────────────┐
│                    Box Town                       │
├─────────────────────────────────────────────────┤
│   Apple Ave.              X                        │
│   ┌───┐    ┌───┐    ┌───┐    ┌───┐    ┌───┐       │
│   │   │    │   │    │   │    │   │    │   │       │
│   └───┘    └───┘    └───┘    └───┘    └───┘       │
│   Baker Ave.                                       │
│   ┌───┐    ┌───┐    ┌───┐    ┌───┐    ┌───┐       │
│   │   │    │   │    │   │    │   │    │   │       │
│   └───┘    └───┘    └───┘    └───┘    └───┘       │
│   Charlie Ave.                                     │
│   ┌───┐    ┌───┐    ┌───┐    ┌───┐    ┌───┐       │
│   │   │    │   │    │   │    │   │    │   │       │
│   └───┘    └───┘    └───┘    └───┘    └───┘       │
│   O   Dark Ave.                                    │
└─────────────────────────────────────────────────┘
   1st      2nd      3rd      4th      5th      6th
   St.      St.      St.      St.      St.      St.
```

```
              N
              │
     W ───────┼─────── E
              │
              S
```

Use dots (...) to draw a path from Point O to Point X.
Now describe the path.

First I went _____blocks _____(direction)

Then I went_____blocks _____(direction)

29.

```
┌─────────────────────────────────────────────────┐
│                    Centertown                     │
├─────────────────────────────────────────────────┤
│                  Apple Ave.                       │
│   ┌───┐      ┌───┐    ┌───┐      ┌───┐    ┌───┐   │
│   │   │      │   │    │   │      │   │    │   │   │
│   └───┘      └───┘    └───┘      └───┘    └───┘   │
│                  Banana Ave.                      │
│   ┌───┐      ┌───┐    ┌───┐      ┌───┐    ┌───┐   │
│   │   │      │   │    │   │      │   │    │   │   │
│   └───┘      └───┘    └───┘      └───┘    └───┘   │
│      O          Carrot Ave.                       │
│   ┌───┐      ┌───┐    ┌───┐      ┌───┐    ┌───┐   │
│   │   │      │   │    │   │      │   │    │   │   │
│   └───┘      └───┘    └───┘      └───┘    └───┘   │
│            Date Ave.        X                     │
└─────────────────────────────────────────────────┘
```

| 1st | 2nd | 3rd | 4th | 5th | 6th |
| St. | St. | St. | St. | St. | St. |

```
            N
            |
    W ──────┼────── E
            |
            S
```

Use dots (...) to draw a path from Point O to Point X.
Now describe the path. See if you can do it without
any hints.

_____

_____

_____

STIC TASK

We'll be getting together again soon, and there will be chances to gain more points. For next time you can earn points for remembering what we did today. OK?

Just in case you're not sure, what we did today was to go slowly and read carefully so we could <u>follow directions</u>. If you can remember that for our next meeting, you'll earn points for your "Show That I Can" (STIC) task. Remember what we did today, I'll ask you about it next time, and you'll earn extra points if you can tell me. OK?

HOW DID YOU DO TODAY?

Go on to the next page, listen to your therapist's explanation of how you'll use the "How did you do today" chart, and then go on to bank your earnings.

HOW DID YOU DO TODAY?

Your rating:	1	2	3	4	5
	Not So Hot	O.K.	Good	Very Good	Super
Therapist's rating:	1	2	3	4	5

Do the ratings agree (within 1 point)?
If they do, you get 2 points!   + _____

Did you remember to do your STIC task?
If you did you get 2 points!   + _____

How many points do you have left
from today?   + _____

Number of points in the bank: + _____
                                                     _____

                                        Total   _____

```
┌─────────────────────────────────────────────────┐
│                   BANK TIME!                      │
│                                                   │
│   You can now spend points, or Bank them for use  │
│   later. That way you can save up for bigger      │
│   prizes!                                         │
│                                                   │
│              Total from above        _____      │
│                                                   │
│    Cost of prize, if you picked one  - _____    │
│                                        _____    │
│                                                   │
│    Total left to go back to the bank   _____    │
│                                                   │
│                                                   │
│   Go now to page 113.  BE SURE TO RECORD YOUR     │
│   TOTAL IN THE BANK.  Save up your points--       │
│   you'll be able spend them at a later time.      │
└─────────────────────────────────────────────────┘
```

SESSION 3: MULTIPLE TASKS

3

Hi again! Let's start off by checking to
see if you remembered the STIC task.

Last session I said I'd ask you today to
remember what we had worked on when we met
last time. Well, here we are! Now if you can tell
me what we did last week, you'll earn the extra
points.

What did we work on at our last meeting? Take your
time and think. Write in your answer below.

_____

_____

Today we're going to work on a whole bunch of
different tasks. Before we start, get out your stop
sign with the steps on it. Let's go over them. Do
you remember them?

We'll be going over the steps many times. For the
first few problems we do today, say the steps out
loud as you do them. Now look at the problems
below, read the directions, and do each task. Be
sure to say the steps out loud.

OPPOSITE AND SIMILAR

1. Read the words below and fill in a word that
means the opposite of each one. The first one is
done for you.

night: day   dirty:

new: whisper:

light: awake:

down: smile:

kind: easy:

soft: distant:

2.   Read the words below and, after each one, fill
in another word that has a similar meaning.   The
first one is done to help you get started.

big: large   thin:

difficult: loud:

depart: wealthy:

wet: relax:

final: correct:

3.   Read the words below.   After each word in the
first column write a word that has a similar
meaning.   After each word in the second column write
a word that means its opposite:

small: brave:

healthy: help:

weak: rivalry:

hot: repair:

stop: rough:

4.   Read the words below.   For each word that begins
with a letter in the **first half** of the alphabet,
write a word that means its **opposite**.   For each word
that begins with a letter in the **second half** of the
alphabet, write a word that has a **similar meaning**.
What do you think would be a good idea to help with
the task?   Try to think of one yourself (you may go
to the bottom of page 29 for an idea).

energetic: in:

future: friend:

begin: thief:

easy: young:

5. Look at the shapes in the table below. Decide if the information at the top of each column is correct and write "right" if it is. If the information is not correct, write "wrong" in the space. The first one is completed to help get you started.

	CIRCLE	TRIANGLE
△	*wrong*	*right*
○	*right*	*wrong*

6. Now try the next one...it is a bit harder. One row is finished to help get you started.

	Not white	Striped	Circle	Not 4-sided	Round and not striped
▲	*right*	*Wrong*	*Wrong*	*right*	*Wrong*
▦					
⊖					
◨					
○					
●					
△					

Good! Let's try some others. Remember to say the steps when doing each task. For the next ones you can whisper the steps.

ALIKE AND DIFFERENT

7. Read the pairs of words below. For all pairs with an **even number**, write one way the words are **alike**. For all word pairs with an **odd number**, write the way the words are **different**.

Before you start, can you think of a helpful plan? Would it help to write "S" for same or "D" for different next to each of the word pairs? You might do that first, then go back and provide the answers.

ball/bat (4)

cat/dog (9)

lemon/banana (77)

spaghetti/carrot (8)

TV/radio (243)

ant/elephant (87)

piano/guitar (88)

anger/joy (5)

glove/mitten (1)

dime/dollar (102)

hear/see (84)

8. The groups of 3 words below are alike in some way. Write a way you think they are alike.

EXAMPLE: firecracker, dynamite, volcano:
    "these can all explode"

circus, zoo, museum: _____

walk, trot, gallop:_____

coin, bill, check:_____

average, common, ordinary:_____

clear, sunny, cloudy:_____

sign, map, address:_____

policeman, mailman, nurse:_____

refrigerator, stove, picnic basket:_____

pin, thread, scissors:_____

YOUR STIC TASK FOR NEXT TIME...

When we get together next time we'll check to see that you can say the steps without looking at the stop sign. Try it now.

Let's practice once more.

OK, you can do it. If you can say the steps next meeting, then you'll earn the bonus points.

HINT FOR PROBLEM #4: Write out the letters of the alphabet and divide the list in half. Then write "Opposite" over the first half and "Similar" over the second half.

HOW DID YOU DO TODAY?

Your rating:	1	2	3	4	5
	Not So Hot	O.K.	Good	Very Good	Super
Therapist's rating:	1	2	3	4	5

Do the ratings agree (within 1 point)?
If they do, you get 2 points!   + _____

Did you remember to do your STIC task?
If you did you get 2 points!   + _____

How many points do you have left
from today?   + _____

Number of points in the bank: + _____
                                                  _____

                                    Total   _____

BANK TIME!

You can now spend points, or Bank them for use later. That way you can save up for bigger prizes!

                 Total from above   _____

    Cost of prize, if you picked one   - _____
                                          _____

    Total left to go back to the bank   _____

Go now to page 113. BE SURE TO RECORD YOUR TOTAL IN THE BANK. Save up your points-- you'll be able spend them at a later time.

30

SESSION 4: ARITHMETIC

Welcome back! Today we are going to look
at some arithmetic problems. But first
can you remember what we do first?

Today, as every time we meet, you can earn
some points for remembering and having done
your STIC task. This time if you can say the steps,
you can earn the extra points. Give it a try.

1 _____

2 _____

3 _____

4 _____

5 _____

Today, we get to practice the steps that you've written while doing schoolwork. You'll show me how you can do it.

Directions: For this task, you'll need your stop sign and a pencil.

Now, look at all these problems. There are a lot of them, aren't there? Well, don't rush. The goal is to learn to do some of the problems correctly, not just to rush and finish. It doesn't matter if you don't finish them all. We're going to do them slowly and correctly. Speed doesn't count here.

For each problem, read each of the steps on the card (on the back of your stop sign) and do each portion of the problem step by step. Say each instruction out loud at first, so you can show your therapist that you know them.

Once your therapist has seen that you can use the steps, then you can whisper the instructions to yourself as you do each step of the problem. Your therapist will let you know when you can whisper.

Sometimes, you'll be able to figure out the problem. When you can, write the answer in the space beside the problem. Have your therapist check the answer. Don't forget to praise yourself when you get the right answer. Sometimes the problems will be too hard for you, because they call for things you have never seen before. When they are too tough, write "NL" ("I have Not Learned this yet") beside the problem. If you and your therapist agree, you can make up some of your own problems. Remember to praise yourself, because identifying what you haven't learned yet is the right answer for such a problem!

Remember! Take your time, do your best, and remember to STOP AND THINK!

STAY ON
TARGET!

4 + 5 = _____   5 - 4 = _____

3 + 3 = _____   3 - 3 = _____

6 + 4 = _____   6 - 4 = _____

12 + 6 = _____   12 - 6 = _____

11 + 8 = _____   11 - 8 = _____

18 + 4 = _____   18 - 4 = _____


```
  26        52        36        55        77
 +31       +17       +18       +30       +18
```


```
  31        52        36        55        77
 -26       -17       -18       -30       -18
```


Can you fill in the missing numbers?

```
   3 8 _        _ 5 _        6 0 7
 +  _ 6      +  5 _ 2     +  _ _ 5
 --------     --------     --------
   3 9 8        9 8 9      1,0 4 2


   _ 0 _        _ _ _        8 _ 8
 +  5 _ 9     +  9 6 7     +  _ 6 _
 --------     --------     --------
 1,0 5 2      1,2 9 5      1,6 6 7
```

2 x 1 = _____   2 / 1 = _____

3 x 2 = _____   4 / 2 = _____

4 x 5 = _____   9 / 3 = _____

3 x 3 = _____   3 / 3 = _____

6 x 4 = _____   6 / 2 = _____


```
  12              11              18
 x 6             x 8             x 4
```

```
6 | 12          8 | 48          3 | 18
```

```
  26        52          36          55        77
 x31       x17         x18         x30       x18
```

```
11 | 176        20 | 620        17 | 901
```

```
24 | 756        13 | 1430       18 | 1947
```

34

$ 61.03 $ 13.50 $ 44.44
− 8.16   + 27.28   + 88.88

1 / 2 hour = _____ minutes.

1 / 4 of a dollar = _____ cents.

1 week = _____ days.

1 / 2 day = _____ hours.

$1 \frac{1}{2} = \frac{}{2}$ $\frac{1}{2} + \frac{1}{2} = $ _____

$\frac{1}{8} + \frac{2}{8} = $ ---- $\frac{1}{3} + \frac{2}{3} = $ ----

$\frac{2}{3} + \frac{2}{3} = $ ---- $\frac{3}{8} + \frac{7}{8} = $ ----

$\frac{1}{8} + \frac{1}{4} = $ ---- $\frac{3}{5} + \frac{1}{10} = $ ----

$\frac{4}{3} + \frac{4}{6} = $ _____ $1 \frac{1}{2} + 2 \frac{1}{2} = $ _____

$4 \frac{2}{5} + 3 \frac{2}{5} = $ _____ $6 \frac{7}{8} + 8 \frac{3}{8} = $ _____

$$4 \frac{5}{6}$$
$$2 \frac{1}{3}$$
$$+6 \frac{1}{6}$$

$$3 \frac{1}{8}$$
$$6 \frac{7}{8}$$
$$+4 \frac{3}{4}$$

$$6 \frac{1}{2}$$
$$8 \frac{2}{3}$$
$$+7 \frac{5}{6}$$

2 / 3 of 33 = _____   1 / 2 of 18 = _____

$\frac{3}{5}$ of 45 = _____ $\frac{2}{9}$ of 81 = _____

Would you like to create some of your own math problems? Use the space below. Ask your therapist to do some of them with you.

FOR NEXT TIME...

Your STIC task for our next meeting is to think of an instance in class or school where you could <u>use</u> the steps. When you come back for your next session tell your therapist how you used the steps at school.

See you next time!

HOW DID YOU DO TODAY?

Your rating:	1	2	3	4	5
	Not So Hot	O.K.	Good	Very Good	Super
Therapist's rating:	1	2	3	4	5

Do the ratings agree (within 1 point)?
If they do, you get 2 points!   + _____

Did you remember to do your STIC task?
If you did you get 2 points!   + _____

How many points do you have left
from today?   + _____

Number of points in the bank: + _____
                                                  _____

                                   Total   _____

```
┌──────────────────────────────────────────────────────┐
│                     BANK TIME!                         │
│                                                        │
│  You can now spend points, or Bank them for use        │
│  later. That way you can save up for bigger            │
│  prizes!                                               │
│                                                        │
│            Total from above        _____             │
│                                                        │
│    Cost of prize, if you picked one  - _____         │
│                                      _____     │
│                                                        │
│  Total left to go back to the bank   _____           │
│                                                        │
│                                                        │
│  Go now to page 113.  BE SURE TO RECORD YOUR           │
│  TOTAL IN THE BANK.  Save up your points--             │
│  you'll be able spend them at a later time.            │
└──────────────────────────────────────────────────────┘
```

SESSION 5: WHICH IS LESS? WHICH IS MORE?

I'm glad you're back! It's good to see you again. Today, we're going to do a numbers game. It's called "Which is less? Which is more?". I'll tell you about the game in a minute. But first, do you remember what we do at the start of each session?

That's right, your STIC task. This time, you can earn extra points if you can tell me a time that it would be a good idea to use the steps at school. What did you think of? Did you do a good job? If you think you did and your therapist agrees you get 2 points!

In today's session, we're going to be comparing things to see which is the bigger of the two, or which one is the smaller of the two. Turn ahead and look at some of the problems. They all ask you a question at the beginning: either "Which is less?" or "Which is more?". Then, the question will list two things or two groups of things, separated by "or". Your job is to compare everything on one side of the "or" to everything on the other side, then answer the question "Which is more?" or "Which is less?". When you have figured it out, circle the correct answer.

Remember, it's not important how many of these you do--No need to rush! It's OK not to finish, as long as you take your time and do the problems correctly, <u>Step-by-Step</u>.

So, sharpen your pencil, get out your stop sign with the steps on it, and let's start the task. Go slowly, do your best, remember...

STOP AND _____

If some of the questions are too easy or too difficult, talk with your therapist and select the level of task that is just right for you.

```
Which is more:        8   or   6 ?

           less:      8        6

           more:      3        9


Which is more:       16   or  20 ?

           less:     31       38

           less:     20       17


Which is more:      316   or 198

           less:     418      611

           more:     940      265
```

Which is less money: one nickel or one dime?

Which is more money: one quarter or one penny?

Which is more money: one penny or one quarter?

Which is less money: two pennies or one nickel?

Which is less money: two nickels or one quarter?

Which is more money: two quarters   or one dime?

Which is less money: three nickels or two dimes?

Which is more money: eight dimes or four quarters?

Which is more in Roman Numerals: V or II ?

Which is less in Roman Numerals: X or VII ?

Which is more in Roman Numerals: XI or IX ?

Which is less in Roman Numerals: CX or XC ?

Which is less: 1   or $\frac{1}{4}$?

Which is less: $\frac{1}{8}$ or $\frac{1}{16}$?

Which is more: $\frac{1}{4}$ or $\frac{3}{4}$?

Which is more: $\frac{3}{5}$ or $\frac{4}{5}$?

Which is more: $\frac{3}{8}$ or $\frac{1}{4}$?

Which is less: $\frac{3}{16}$ or $\frac{1}{8}$?

Which is more: $1\frac{3}{4}$ or $\frac{1}{4}$?

Which is more: $2\frac{3}{5}$ or $2\frac{4}{5}$?

Which is less: $1\frac{1}{2}$ or $1\frac{3}{4}$?

Which is less: $7\frac{3}{8}$ or $7\frac{1}{2}$?

Which is more: $\frac{5}{3}$ or $1\frac{1}{3}$?

Which is more: two dimes and a penny, or...

        two dimes and a nickel ?

Which is less: three pennies and a dime, or...

        three pennies and a quarter ?

Which is less: four dimes and a nickel, or...

        four nickels and a dime ?

Which is less: two quarters and a penny, or...

two pennies and a quarter ?

Which is more: 6 pennies and a nickel, or...

6 nickels and a penny ?

Which is less: 2 dimes and 3 nickels, or...

3 dimes and 2 nickels ?

Which is more: 4 dimes and six pennies, or...

six dimes and 4 pennies ?

Which is more: 2 quarters and 3 dimes, or...

3 quarters and 2 dimes ?

Which is more: five nickels and two quarters, or...

two nickels and 5 quarters ?

Which is more: 3 nickels and 4 dimes, or...

one quarter and 6 nickels ?

Which is less: 18 pennies and 2 quarters, or...

3 nickels and 6 dimes ?

Which is more: three quarters and 20 pennies, or...

6 dimes and 7 nickels ?

Which is less: 4 nickels and 2 dimes, or...

2 pennies and 4 quarters ?

Can you create some problems like the ones you've just finished? Try to write in a few and ask your therapist to do them with you.

FOR NEXT SESSION...

Your STIC task for next session is this: between now and the next session, use your problem-solving steps to solve some problem at school. Then, at your next session, tell your therapist how you did. OK ?

This STIC task is a little different from the ones we've done so far. It's not enough just to think of the steps. This time, you are to actually use the steps. Then, you get the points for telling your therapist about how you used the steps and how the situation turned out.

To make sure you understand, tell your therapist what the STIC task is for next time.

So long for now. See you soon.

HOW DID YOU DO TODAY?

Your rating:	1	2	3	4	5
		Not So Hot	O.K.	Good	Very Good	Super
Therapist's rating:	1	2	3	4	5

Do the ratings agree (within 1 point)?
If they do, you get 2 points!   + _____

Did you remember to do your STIC task?
If you did you get 2 points!   + _____

How many points do you have left
from today?   + _____

Number of points in the bank: + _____
                                                    _____

                                        Total   _____

BANK TIME!

You can now spend points, or Bank them for use
later. That way you can save up for bigger
prizes!

                    Total from above   _____

    Cost of prize, if you picked one   -   _____
                                            _____

    Total left to go back to the bank   _____

Go now to page 113. BE SURE TO RECORD YOUR
TOTAL IN THE BANK. Save up your points--
you'll be able spend them at a later time.

SESSION 6: WORD SEARCH

Howdy! Before we start today let's see how you did with your STIC task from last week.

Take a minute now and think of a time at school when you used the steps. Tell your therapist about it.

If you did a good job you earned two points!

Today we're going to try some word puzzles. Get out your stop sign and your magnifying glass. Remember, there may be times that we need to slow down and use the steps on the back of your stop sign.

Have you ever done word search puzzles? If you haven't, don't worry. The task is easy if you go slowly and take your time. All you have to do is find the words among the letters.

To focus in on the letters and rows, you can use your magnifying glass. <u>Focus In</u> on a row. Place the magnifying glass over the puzzle so that you can only see one row at a time. This will help you to <u>focus</u>. Think ahead, what strategy will you use to search and find the words? Talk it over with your therapist. How will you keep track of the words you've found?

```
P   C   H   I   C   K   E   N
I   R   C   T   P   S   C   H
Z   A   E   L   A   M   A   O
Z   P   R   T   S   O   N   T
A   P   E   O   Z   R   D   D
X   L   A   S   A   E   Y   O
J   E   L   L   O   S   L   G
T   C   A   R   R   O   T   S
```

————————————————

FUN
FOODS

PIZZA   JELLO

HOTDOGS   CARROTS

CEREAL   CHICKEN

PRETZELS   S'MORES

APPLE   CANDY

```
P  P  A  C  M  A  N  N

R  A  D  L  E  Z  C  H

O  D  R  A  G  O  N  G

J  E  O  P  A  R  D  Y

L  G  I  M  A  R  I  O

I  O  S  I  R  T  E  T

N  L  T  O  P  G  U  N

K  F  K  U  N  G  F  U
```

NINTENDO GAMES

TOPGUN	PACMAN
JEOPARDY	LINK
(super)MARIO	ZELDA
(double)DRAGON	GOLF
KUNG—FU	TETRIS

```
G   A   M   E   S   S   M   M
X   S   T   F   A   R   C   I
T   T   R   I   B   L   R   D
I   I   B   O   O   T   H   W
C   R   O   W   D   S   F   A
K   K   N   T   O   U   O   Y
E   S   E   D   I   R   O   E
T   C   I   S   U   M   D   E
```

AT
THE
FAIR

BOOTH   MIDWAY

CLOWNS   CRAFTS

TICKET   RIDES

MUSIC   CROWDS

GAMES   FOOD

Want to make your own? Use the space below to make
your own word searches.

YOUR STIC TASK FOR NEXT TIME

Check the title of our next session.
"Bring your own", that's right. Want to know more
about it?

For next session, bring in some of your own school
books or school work. You can bring several things,
although we will probably just work on a few of
them. Don't forget!

See you then!

HOW DID YOU DO TODAY?

Your rating:	1	2	3	4	5
	Not So Hot	O.K.	Good	Very Good	Super
Therapist's rating:	1	2	3	4	5

Do the ratings agree (within 1 point)?
If they do, you get 2 points!   + _____

Did you remember to do your STIC task?
If you did you get 2 points!   + _____

How many points do you have left
from today?   + _____

Number of points in the bank: + _____
                                                        _____
                                    Total   _____

```
┌─────────────────────────────────────────────────┐
│                   BANK TIME!                      │
│                                                   │
│  You can now spend points, or Bank them for use   │
│  later. That way you can save up for bigger       │
│  prizes!                                          │
│                                                   │
│              Total from above      _____        │
│                                                   │
│     Cost of prize, if you picked one  - _____   │
│                                        _____  │
│                                                   │
│  Total left to go back to the bank    _____     │
│                                                   │
│                                                   │
│  Go now to page 113.  BE SURE TO RECORD YOUR      │
│  TOTAL IN THE BANK.  Save up your points--        │
│  you'll be able spend them at a later time.       │
└─────────────────────────────────────────────────┘
```

50

SESSION 7: "BRING YOUR OWN"

Today, unlike almost all of our other
meetings, we will be working **outside** your
Stop and Think Workbook. Remember your
STIC task from last time? Did you remember
your school work? I bet you did. Terrific!

Take a few minutes to relax, think about the
steps, and select some of your own schoolwork to
work on with your therapist. Your job for today is
to use your problem-solving steps to complete your
own work from school.

There are many ways to accomplish this. Take
some time to talk with your therapist, to discuss
the various ways you can work, and the several
possible school assignments to focus on. The rules
about Stop and Think Dollars are the same, but the
type of work you do is up to you!

YOUR STIC TASK FOR NEXT TIME

Between today and the next time we meet, use your
problem-solving steps when you identify a problem at
home. It's not enough just to notice the problem...
you have to use the steps to work out a solution.
Can you say what the STIC task is for next time? Go
ahead, repeat the STIC task. Next time you can tell
your therapist how things turned out.

HOW DID YOU DO TODAY?

Your rating:	1	2	3	4	5
	Not So Hot	O.K.	Good	Very Good	Super
Therapist's rating:	1	2	3	4	5

Do the ratings agree (within 1 point)?
If they do, you get 2 points!   + _____

Did you remember to do your STIC task?
If you did you get 2 points!   + _____

How many points do you have left
from today?   + _____

Number of points in the bank: + _____
                                                    _____

                                          Total   _____

```
┌─────────────────────────────────────────────────────┐
│                      BANK TIME!                       │
│                                                       │
│   You can now spend points, or Bank them for use      │
│   later. That way you can save up for bigger          │
│   prizes!                                             │
│                                                       │
│                    Total from above      _____      │
│                                                       │
│     Cost of prize, if you picked one    - _____     │
│                                           _____ │
│                                                       │
│   Total left to go back to the bank       _____     │
│                                                       │
│                                                       │
│   Go now to page 113.  BE SURE TO RECORD YOUR         │
│   TOTAL IN THE BANK.  Save up your points--           │
│   you'll be able spend them at a later time.          │
└─────────────────────────────────────────────────────┘
```

SOMETHING TO CROW ABOUT!

52

SESSION 8: CHECKERS

Today you get to take it easy! The task for
today is to play a few games of checkers.
It should be fun. Once again, we will use
the steps...but before we play...

Recall your STIC task? Tell your therapist
about a time when you used the steps to solve a
problem you were having while at school.

Before we play checkers, or any game, we need to
know the rules. So, let's agree on the rules before
we begin.   Below you will find some rules to
consider. After you and your therapist discuss the
rules and agree on the rules that you will play by,
you may begin the games.

---

1. The checkers go on the black squares.

2. The person with the black checkers goes first.

3. You move your checkers one square forward
   diagonally along the black squares of the
   checkerboard. You can't go backwards until
   your piece is a king!

4. Some people play by the rule that if one of
   your opponents pieces can be jumped
   you **must** jump the piece...and if there are
   several successive jumps, then you must make
   all of them. Consider this possible rule.
   Decide **before** the game if you want to use
   it.

5. If one of your pieces gets all the way across
   the board, it turns into a king. Put another
   piece on top of it to indicate that it is a
   king. A king is like any other piece except
   that it can move in any direction along the
   black squares.

6. If you take your finger off of your piece,
   then the move counts. Don't take your finger
   off the piece unless you are sure of the move.

7. Any other rules that you decide on beforehand.

STIC TASK

Think of a time when it would be a good idea to use the steps when playing a game. Also, think of several games where it would be a good idea to use the steps. Tell your therapist at the start of next session, and you'll earn the bonus points.

HOW DID YOU DO TODAY?

Your rating:	1	2	3	4	5
	Not So Hot	O.K.	Good	Very Good	Super
Therapist's rating:	1	2	3	4	5

Do the ratings agree (within 1 point)?
If they do, you get 2 points!   + _____

Did you remember to do your STIC task?
If you did you get 2 points!   + _____

How many points do you have left
from today?   + _____

Number of points in the bank: + _____
                                                     _____

                                         Total   _____

```
+-------------------------------------------------------+
|                   BANK TIME!                          |
|                                                       |
|   You can now spend points, or Bank them for use      |
|   later. That way you can save up for bigger          |
|   prizes!                                             |
|                                                       |
|              Total from above       _____           |
|                                                       |
|     Cost of prize, if you picked one  - _____       |
|                                         _____       |
|                                                       |
|    Total left to go back to the bank    _____       |
|                                                       |
|                                                       |
|   Go now to page 113.  BE SURE TO RECORD YOUR         |
|   TOTAL IN THE BANK.  Save up your points--           |
|   you'll be able spend them at a later time.          |
+-------------------------------------------------------+
```

SESSION 9: CAT AND MOUSE

How are you today? Do you remember your
STIC task for today? Let's check. The
task was (1) to tell your therapist about
a time when playing a game that it would
be a good idea to use the steps, and (2)
to tell your therapist about some game
where it would be good to use the steps.

Today we're going to play a game that you've
probably never played before. It's called "Cat and
Mouse." For this game you'll need:

1. a checkerboard
2. 1 black checker
3. 4 red checkers

The black checker is the "mouse." It tries to avoid
the "cats" (the red checkers) as they move across
the board. Before we play the game, however, let's
learn the rules.

Rules for "Cat and Mouse"

1. The black checker (the mouse) is placed in
   the middle red square on one side of the
   board.

2. The four red checkers (the cats) are placed
   on the four red squares on the opposite
   side of the board.

3. The mouse moves first. It can move one
   square in any direction on any of the red
   squares.

4. One cat can move each turn. The cats may
   only move forward; never backward.

5. Neither the cats nor the mouse may jump.

6. The game is over either when the mouse gets
   past the cats, or when the cats surround or
   corner the mouse so that it cannot move.

Before starting, have each player try to say the rules without looking at them. After a game or two of "Cat and Mouse" you and your therapist can think of another game to play. Be sure to agree on the rules before you begin. Make a list of the rules so that you don't forget them.

Have fun! We'll see you next time.

YOUR STIC TASK FOR NEXT TIME...

Two STIC tasks for next time.   (1). There are problems that happen when playing.   For next session, your STIC task is to use the steps to help solve a problem that started when you were playing. Here's a hint, problems in games may involve taking turns, accidental bumps that mess up the board, someone who cheats, etc. Your job is to remember to stop and think during a game and to tell your therapist next time.   (2) Bring a magazine to the next session.

HOW DID YOU DO TODAY?

Your rating:	1	2	3	4	5
	Not So Hot	O.K.	Good	Very Good	Super
Therapist's rating:	1	2	3	4	5

Do the ratings agree (within 1 point)?
If they do, you get 2 points!   + _____

Did you remember to do your STIC task?
If you did you get 2 points!   + _____

How many points do you have left
from today?   + _____

Number of points in the bank: + _____
                                                     _____

                                        Total   _____

```
┌─────────────────────────────────────────────────┐
│                   BANK TIME!                      │
│                                                   │
│   You can now spend points, or Bank them for use  │
│   later. That way you can save up for bigger      │
│   prizes!                                          │
│                                                   │
│              Total from above        _____       │
│                                                   │
│     Cost of prize, if you picked one  -  _____   │
│                                       _____ │
│                                                   │
│   Total left to go back to the bank   _____      │
│                                                   │
│                                                   │
│   Go now to page 113.  BE SURE TO RECORD YOUR     │
│   TOTAL IN THE BANK.  Save up your points--        │
│   you'll be able spend them at a later time.      │
└─────────────────────────────────────────────────┘
```

SESSION 10: RECOGNIZING FEELINGS

10

Before we start, be sure to discuss your STIC task with your therapist. Tell your therapist about a time that you were playing a game and used the steps to solve a problem that occurred during the game. Did you do a good job? If you did, terrific. If you tried, but it didn't work out, that's OK. Talk with your therapist about how to have alternate plans ready in case the first plan doesn't work out. Did you bring your magazine?

Today we will have some fun learning about different feelings that people have.

I'll bet you can name 4 different feelings that people have. Write them in the spaces below.

1. _____

2. _____

3. _____

4. _____

Some feelings "feel" good ("feel good" feelings). Some make you feel bad, and we call those "feel bad" feelings. Some feelings are "in-between" good and bad: not really good or bad. Look at the 5 feelings that you wrote. What kind of feelings are they? Put them in one of the boxes below.

FEEL GOOD	IN-BETWEEN	FEEL BAD

Can you add a few more feelings for each box? Look at the list below and add them to the boxes. Use a dictionary if you would like.

Excited	Embarrassed	Joyful
Surprised	Pleased	Calm
Scared	Shy	Jealous
Bored	Content	Upset
Proud	Bitter	Mean

OK, now that you are thinking about feelings, here's a question for you:

How do people show their feelings? Can you think of two ways? Write them in below.

1. _____

2. _____

People show their feelings in their faces and in their bodies.

Let's think about how people show feelings in their faces. Like Detective Dan, let's try to figure out what feeling each face is showing. Use your list of feelings for some ideas.

_____   _____

_____   _____

You've just finished naming the feelings that go
with four different faces. Make one of the faces
yourself and see how it feels to you. Pick one for
your therapist to try.

People can determine "feelings" from the context of
stories as well as from facial expressions. Read
the following stories and write in the feeling you
might have. You can draw the face, too, if you'd
like.

1. Your best friend comes running up to you on the
   playground. He says, "Let's go play with my
   basketball!"

What feeling would you have?_____

Draw a face to show that feeling. You can copy a
face from these pages if there is one that "shows"
how you would feel.

2. This week you and your class were very well
   behaved and the teachers decided you could all
   go on the school trip to the zoo. But on the
   day of the trip it is raining so the trip to the
   zoo is canceled.

What feeling would you have?_____

Draw a face to show the feeling.

3. You are home alone and you think you hear a
   noise in the other room.

What feeling would you have?_____

Draw a face to show the feeling.

OK, now let's talk about how people express feelings
with their bodies. You can sometimes show your
feelings in the way you stand or sit, in where you
put your hands, or how you hold your head.

Look at the pictures of people below. Pick one
person from each picture and think about how that
person is feeling. Can you think of several
feelings for the person? List them:

1. _____   1. _____

2. _____   2. _____

3. _____   3. _____

4. _____   4. _____

Did you remember to bring a magazine for today's meeting? If so, take it out now and find pictures of people. Take a look at the people and describe their emotions. If you forgot the magazine, then look at the pictures your therapist is showing you. Name the person and write the feeling that you think the person is showing. You may select more than three, but be sure to do at least three

1. _____

2. _____

3. _____

4. _____

Do you know how to play charades? It's a game where you act, but without speaking. Try to act a feeling. For example, make a sad face to show a sad feeling. Pick a feeling from the list and act it out for your therapist. See how good your therapist is at identifying the feeling. Next, it's your therapist's turn to act out a feeling for you to guess! Use the steps to help solve the problem.

YOUR STIC TASK FOR NEXT TIME...

Bring in 3 pictures of people, taken from a magazine or newspaper, and identify and describe their feelings. Write a short sentence or two for each picture.

See you next time! Don't forget to bring the pictures with you.

HOW DID YOU DO TODAY?

Your rating:	1	2	3	4	5
	Not So Hot	O.K.	Good	Very Good	Super
Therapist's rating:	1	2	3	4	5

Do the ratings agree (within 1 point)?
If they do, you get 2 points!   + _____

Did you remember to do your STIC task?
If you did you get 2 points!   + _____

How many points do you have left
from today?   + _____

Number of points in the bank: + _____
                                                  _____

                                        Total   _____

BANK TIME!

You can now spend points, or Bank them for use later. That way you can save up for bigger prizes!

               Total from above   _____

   Cost of prize, if you picked one   - _____
                                          _____

   Total left to go back to the bank   _____

Go now to page 113. BE SURE TO RECORD YOUR TOTAL IN THE BANK. Save up your points-- you'll be able spend them at a later time.

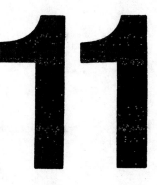

SESSION 11: WHAT AM I FEELING?
WHAT ARE OTHERS FEELING?

Hi again! Did you remember to bring
in the magazine pictures? Tell your
therapist about them. If you did a
good job, you are awarded 2 points!

Today, you will be using the steps to help yourself
understand what people might be feeling.

Are you ready?   What's the problem (task) to
remember? Write it down in the space below.

_____

_____

Right, use the steps to figure out how someone is
feeling. Now, look at the picture below:

What is the boy feeling?_____

What else might he be feeling?_____

Think of a feeling that the parents could have:

_____

How did you do? Ask your therapist.

OK, now let's try the same thing with another picture. What are the kids in the next picture feeling?

He might be feeling_____

She might be feeling_____

OK, let's try a different one! Let's make a picture in our imagination. Ready?

You and a friend have planned to play together today after school. Now pretend that when you get home from school today, your friend calls to say that he/she can't come over to play. Now you have no one to play with. Can you picture that in your imagination? OK, let's imagine that it happened.

How might you feel?_____

Think of one more feeling you might have:

_____

Did you do a good job? Tell yourself!

Pretend that it's Friday, school is over, and you have no homework. Soon your friend, Randy, will be coming over and it will be a lot of fun. You plan to go riding bikes.

How will you feel?_____

What else?_____

And your friend, how might your friend feel?
_____

Did you do a good job? Tell yourself!

Now it's your turn to make up a situation that is all your own. You create a scene and ask your therapist to name 2 or 3 feelings that the person might have. Have your therapist write the feelings in the space below.

1. _____

2. _____

3. _____

What do you think? Did your therapist do a good job?

One last challenge! Name 3 people, or story characters, and assign each one a feeling. Write down their names and feelings below. Ask your therapist to make up a story that involves all 3 people and is accurate to their feelings.

NAME	FEELING

YOUR STIC TASK FOR NEXT TIME:

For next time, think of 2 people and 2 situations:

In one situation they need to go very slowly, and when they do go slowly, they feel really happy.

In the second, the characters are supposed to pay attention and think ahead, but they don't and they're embarrassed.

Remember, 2 people and 2 different situations. Your job is to "think up" the stories. Do you want to write this down so you'll remember? Have your therapist get you a pencil and some paper if you want to write it down.

See you next time!

HOW DID YOU DO TODAY?

Your rating:	1	2	3	4	5
	Not So Hot	O.K.	Good	Very Good	Super
Therapist's rating:	1	2	3	4	5

Do the ratings agree (within 1 point)?
If they do, you get 2 points!   + _____

Did you remember to do your STIC task?
If you did you get 2 points!   + _____

How many points do you have left
from today?   + _____

Number of points in the bank: + _____
                                                   _____

                                          Total   _____

```
┌─────────────────────────────────────────────┐
│                 BANK TIME!                    │
│                                               │
│   You can now spend points, or Bank them for  │
│   use later. That way you can save up for      │
│   bigger prizes!                               │
│                                               │
│               Total from above      _____   │
│                                               │
│      Cost of prize, if you picked one - _____│
│                                       _____│
│                                               │
│   Total left to go back to the bank   _____  │
│                                               │
│                                               │
│   Go now to page 113.  BE SURE TO RECORD YOUR │
│   TOTAL IN THE BANK.  Save up your points--    │
│   you'll be able spend them at a later time.   │
└─────────────────────────────────────────────┘
```

Go now to page 113.

SESSION 12: WHERE DO FEELINGS COME FROM?

Do we have some detective work to do today? You bet we do! We are going to try to figure out what people are feeling and then try to discover why they might have those feelings. We are going to try to be more AWARE of how other people feel and why.

But first things first--did you remember the STIC task? Tell your stories that lead to the different feelings. If you did a good job, award yourself 1 point for each story.

OK, let's get busy! Look at the face below.

What feeling does this face show?_____

What makes people feel that way? Can you think of two reasons why the person in the picture might feel that way?

1. _____

2. _____

Now look at this face.

Can you think of 2 reasons why the person in the picture might feel that way?

1. _____

2. _____

OK, you draw a face now. Pick a feeling and draw how someone with that feeling might look.

Now, can you think of three reasons someone might be feeling that way? List them below:

1. _____

2. _____

3. _____

Was it difficult to think of 3 different reasons? It will become easier with practice. Remember your steps? State the problem, focus in, think of some possibilities...That's it, you've got it.

Well, now that you have had some practice, let's try some detective work!

Look at the picture below. Take a close look.

What is the boy in this picture feeling?

_____

Why might he be feeling that way?

_____

Can you detect 2 other reasons for these feelings?
If you're having problems, take your time, check
with your therapist.

1. _____

2. _____

OK, let's try another one. But first, should we
rush to finish? No. Let's be sure we take our time
and do a good job. If you need to, you can finish
the work during the next session. Check the time,
think ahead, and make a plan with your therapist. If
you finish being a "feelings detective" for all of
the pictures in the workbook, you can select other
pictures of people from magazines.

Look at this drawing:

Look at the person nearest you. How is this person feeling?

_____

Why is this person feeling that way? Think of two possible reasons. Be a thoughtful detective--look at the whole cartoon for clues about why he is feeling that way.

1. _____

2. _____

How are you doing? Check with your therapist. Ok, let's think about this some more. Look at the reasons you wrote down. Is there one that you think is the best answer? Which one do you think is probably the reason for the way that person is feeling? Circle the number that you think is the best answer.

How might the other boys be feeling?

1. _____

2. _____

3. _____

Can you think of two reasons why they feel like that?

1. _____

2. _____

Now read the following story and consider how each person might feel and why.

James and Paul are friends, but James is much better at basketball than Paul. Both boys try out for the basketball team. James makes the A team, which is the best team. Paul makes the B team, which does not have the best players on it.

How is each boy feeling? Think of 2 reasons for James' feelings. Which one might be the most likely reason for his feelings? Now do the same for Paul.

Reasons for James' feelings	Reasons for Paul's feelings
1. _____	_____
2. _____	_____

Here's another story.

Jason felt very tired when he woke up. Then he had a fight with his mother about getting out of bed and about what clothes he was going to wear. Jason's friend, Brian, had a good night's sleep and had fun with his mother before getting on the school bus. When Brian saw Jason on the playground that morning, he ran over and asked Jason to play a game. But Jason just yelled at Brian and ran away.

Now, let's do some detective work (see next page). How might each boy be feeling? Think of 2 reasons for these feelings. Think it over, and then decide which reason is the most likely one for each boy's feelings. Circle the number of the reason that you think fits the story the best.

77

Name	Feeling		Reason
Jason	_____	1.	_____
		2.	_____
Brian	_____	1.	_____
		2.	_____

YOUR STIC TASK FOR NEXT WEEK:

The STIC task for next time is to watch people and try to guess how they are feeling and why. You can do it with characters in a T.V. show, a movie, or with people at the mall. For next time, tell your therapist about a situation, about how a person in the situation was acting and feeling, and why.

HOW DID YOU DO TODAY?

Your rating:	1	2	3	4	5
	Not So Hot	O.K.	Good	Very Good	Super
Therapist's rating:	1	2	3	4	5

Do the ratings agree (within 1 point)?
If they do, you get 2 points!   + _____

Did you remember to do your STIC task?
If you did you get 2 points!   + _____

How many points do you have left
from today?   + _____

Number of points in the bank: + _____

                                                   _____

                                      Total   _____

```
┌─────────────────────────────────────────────────┐
│                   BANK TIME!                      │
│                                                   │
│  You can now spend points, or Bank them for use   │
│  later. That way you can save up for bigger       │
│  prizes!                                          │
│                                                   │
│              Total from above      _____        │
│                                                   │
│     Cost of prize, if you picked one  -  _____  │
│                                       _____  │
│                                                   │
│  Total left to go back to the bank    _____     │
│                                                   │
│                                                   │
│  Go now to page 113.  BE SURE TO RECORD YOUR      │
│  TOTAL IN THE BANK.  Save up your points--        │
│  you'll be able spend them at a later time.       │
└─────────────────────────────────────────────────┘
```

SESSION 13: WHAT WOULD HAPPEN IF?

13

Before we start today let's go over your STIC task from last session. Your STIC task was to figure out why somebody might have been feeling the way that they did. Tell your therapist about what you've done. If you did a good job, you'll earn 2 points!

Today we're going to do detective work on the case "what would happen if?" As a detective you have to figure out what the problem is and what to do about it. We'll use the steps.

First read the cases below, and then select one. Don't rush. Read them all before you pick one.

> 1. You are working on your homework and your friend starts talking to you.
>
> 2. You are watching television and one of your family members changes the channel.
>
> 3. You tear your pants during a break at school and someone makes fun of you.
>
> 4. Your friend walks by your desk and knocks your book off as he/or she goes by.
>
> 5. You are playing checkers and the kid you are playing with is cheating.

What number did you choose? Write it here. _____

Let's use the steps to solve the problem.

FIRST: You need to stop and think for a minute: What is the problem here? Write it down in your own words.

_____

_____

SECOND: What are some possible things you could do?

1. One is_____

2. Another could be_____

3. Another could be_____

THIRD: Focus in on each possibility. Ask yourself: "What might happen if I chose my first solution?"

_____

"How would I feel?"

_____

"How would the other person feel?"

_____

"What might the other person do?"

_____

Ask yourself:
"What would happen if I chose my second solution?"

_____

"How would I feel?"

_____

"How would the other person feel?"

_____

"What might the other person do?"

_____

Ask yourself:
"What would happen if I chose my third solution?"

_____

"How would I feel?"

_____

"How would the other person feel?"

_____

"What might the other person do?"

_____

FOURTH: After thinking through all the possibilities, which one would you want to do? Which one is the best solution for you? Write it down, briefly, below.

_____

FIFTH: How do you think you did?

Very good--if so, tell yourself.

Not so hot--if so, take your time, you can rethink the problem.

In any case, you did good work trying to think through all the steps!

Now, turn back to the first page of this session and pick another problem to solve. What number did you select? Write it down here. _____

FIRST: Stop and think for a minute: What is the problem here? Write it down.

_____

_____

SECOND: Ask yourself: "What are the possible things
I could do?"

1. One is_____

2. Another could be_____

3. Another could be_____

THIRD: Focus in on each possibility.

Ask yourself:
"What would happen if I chose my first solution?"

_____

"How would I feel?"

_____

"How would the other person feel?"

_____

"What might the other person do?"

_____

Ask yourself:
"What would happen if I chose my second solution?"

_____

"How would I feel?"

_____

"How would the other person feel?"

_____

"What might the other person do?"

_____

Ask yourself:
"What would happen if I chose my third solution?"

_____

"How would I feel?"

_____

"How would the other person feel?"

_____

"What might the other person do?"

_____

FOURTH: After thinking through all the possibilities, what do you think is a good solution? Write it in your own words, briefly.

_____

FIFTH: How do you think you did?

 Very good--if so, tell yourself.

 Not so hot--if so, take your time, you can do better next time.

GOOD WORK USING THE STEPS!

YOUR STIC TASK FOR NEXT TIME:

For next time, identify a problem that involves you and someone else. Identify the problem, think of 3 alternative solutions and think of how you and the other person would feel about each possible solution. When you meet with your therapist next time you can earn points by telling how you thought through the problem.

See you then. Bye!

HOW DID YOU DO TODAY?

Your rating:	1	2	3	4	5
	Not So Hot	O.K.	Good	Very Good	Super
Therapist's rating:	1	2	3	4	5

Do the ratings agree (within 1 point)?
If they do, you get 2 points!   + _____

Did you remember to do your STIC task?
If you did you get 2 points!   + _____

How many points do you have left
from today?   + _____

Number of points in the bank: + _____
                                                  _____

                                         Total   _____

BANK TIME!

You can now spend points, or Bank them for use later. That way you can save up for bigger prizes!

                    Total from above   _____

    Cost of prize, if you picked one   -   _____
                                           _____

    Total left to go back to the bank   _____

Go now to page 113. BE SURE TO RECORD YOUR
TOTAL IN THE BANK. Save up your points--
you'll be able spend them at a later time.

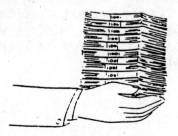

SESSION 14: WHAT WOULD HAPPEN IF?
Part II

Hello again! Can you guess what
we're going to do first? Yes, we're
going to see how you did on the STIC
task. Remember what your STIC task
was? Tell your therapist about your
STIC task...and when you're done, give yourself
a pat on the back!

This time, like last session, we have some problems
for you to solve. But, this time you will write in
the steps yourself! Try to do it on your own, but
you can check back to last session if you need a
little help. Here are the new cases:

---

1. You are having trouble with a worksheet and
   your friend has already finished it.

2. You promised your friend something, but
   later you can't give it to him/her.

3. You say the wrong answer in class and the
   person behind you starts to laugh.

4. You and your friend both want to read the
   same library book, and your friend finds it
   first on the shelf.

5. You are playing ball on the playground and
   when you turn around to talk to a friend
   you get hit in the back with the ball.

Write down the case you have chosen to solve.
Case number_____

Now it is time to use the steps to solve the
problem. Write out your steps as you do them.

What do you do FIRST?

_____

_____

What comes SECOND?

_____

_____

What is the NEXT step?

_____

_____

The NEXT step?

_____

_____

ANYTHING ELSE?

_____

_____

GOOD JOB! YOU HAVE BECOME A GREAT DETECTIVE!

Next, go back to the first page of this session and
pick another case to solve. Case number? _____

What do you do FIRST?

_____

_____

What comes SECOND?

_____

_____

What is the next STEP?

_____

_____

And next?

_____

_____

Anything else?

_____

_____

ANOTHER GOOD JOB! YOU ARE A GREAT DETECTIVE!

YOUR STIC TASK FOR NEXT TIME:

Your STIC task for next time is the same as the one
for today. Identify a problem that involves you and
someone else (e.g., parent, teacher). Identify the
problem, think of 3 alternative solutions and think
of how you and the other person would feel about
each possible solution. When you meet with your
therapist next time you can earn points by telling
how you thought through the problem.

See you next time!

HOW DID YOU DO TODAY?

Your rating:	1	2	3	4	5
	Not So Hot	O.K.	Good	Very Good	Super
Therapist's rating:	1	2	3	4	5

Do the ratings agree (within 1 point)?
If they do, you get 2 points!   + _____

Did you remember to do your STIC task?
If you did you get 2 points!   + _____

How many points do you have left
from today?   + _____

Number of points in the bank: + _____
                                                     _____

                                        Total   _____

BANK TIME!

You can now spend points, or Bank them for use later. That way you can save up for bigger prizes!

                    Total from above   _____

    Cost of prize, if you picked one   - _____
                                             _____

    Total left to go back to the bank   _____

Go now to page 113. BE SURE TO RECORD YOUR TOTAL IN THE BANK. Save up your points-- you'll be able spend them at a later time.

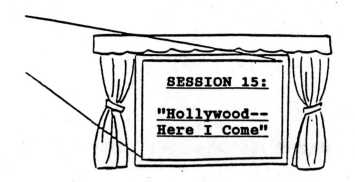

SESSION 15:

"Hollywood--
Here I Come"

Hi again! Remember your STIC task from last week? Tell your therapist what you did and evaluate your problem-solving!

Today we will work on some tasks that are a lot like the ones we did last time, except today we are going to Hollywood--to act out the situations. We will use the steps again, sometimes saying them aloud, other times just saying them silently in our head.

Remember to do what you say to yourself when using the steps. Remember how last time we made up different solutions to each situation? Well, today we will think about the situation, come up with some possible solutions, and think about the consequences of each choice. Then we will act out each possible solution. Later we can pick the one we think is best. For each situation, you will pretend to be one character or person, and your therapist will pretend to be the other person. Don't forget, you can lose points if you go too fast or forget a step.

OK, before we get started, let's get some "situation cards." These are cards that describe situations that we can act out. We need to cut them out from the back of your workbook. Go to back to find them. After you've cut them out, turn them upside down so that you can't see what they say and shuffle them. When you've finished shuffling, just stack them one on the other like a deck of cards.

Ready? OK, turn over the top card and think about how you can act it out with your therapist. When you're ready, and you've thought about what you'll say and do, go ahead and act it out. Be sure to discuss it with your therapist before you get started.

After you give the first one a try, talk it over with your therapist.

"How did you feel?"

"Would the solution you tried be effective?"

Let's go on to the next one. Use the steps as you have been for the last few sessions. After you finish acting out each situation, discuss the performance with your therapist. Then go ahead and try another situation. Have fun!

Lights...Camera...ACTION!

YOUR STIC TASK FOR NEXT TIME:

Your task for next time is the same as the last session. Specify a problem that involves you and someone else. Identify the problem, think of 3 alternative solutions and think of how you and the other person would feel about each possible solution. When you meet with your therapist next time you can earn points by telling how you thought through the problem.

See you next time!

HOW DID YOU DO TODAY?

Your rating:	1	2	3	4	5
	Not So Hot	O.K.	Good	Very Good	Super
Therapist's rating:	1	2	3	4	5

Do the ratings agree (within 1 point)?
If they do, you get 2 points!   + _____

Did you remember to do your STIC task?
If you did you get 2 points!   + _____

How many points do you have left
from today?   + _____

Number of points in the bank: + _____
                                                   _____

                                         Total   _____

BANK TIME!

You can now spend points, or Bank them for use later. That way you can save up for bigger prizes!

Total from above   _____

Cost of prize, if you picked one   - _____
                                           _____

Total left to go back to the bank   _____

Go now to page 113. BE SURE TO RECORD YOUR TOTAL IN THE BANK. Save up your points-- you'll be able spend them at a later time.

SESSION 16:

"Hollywood--
Here I am"!

Hi there! First things first. Go over your STIC task from last session. By now I would bet that you are getting really good at your STIC tasks and at being a problem-solving detective. Keep up the good work!

Today we're going to do something similar to last week, but a little different. This time instead of acting out situations that are on cards, you and your therapist will make up the situations. So, take a minute and talk it over with your therapist. You can think up as many as ten different situations.

Use the blank situation cards at the back of your workbook to write out the ten problem situations. Then, like last week, shuffle them up, stack them face down, pick the top one, and act it out.

Lights...Cameras...ACTION!

YOUR STIC TASK FOR NEXT TIME:

Can you guess the STIC task for next time? That's right...same as the last session. Specify a problem that involves you and someone else. Identify the problem, think of 3 alternative solutions and think of how you and the other person would feel about each possible solution. When you meet with your therapist next time you will describe how you thought through the problem and its solution.

See you next time!

HOW DID YOU DO TODAY?

Your rating:	1	2	3	4	5
	Not So Hot	O.K.	Good	Very Good	Super
Therapist's rating:	1	2	3	4	5

Do the ratings agree (within 1 point)?
If they do, you get 2 points!   + _____

Did you remember to do your STIC task?
If you did you get 2 points!   + _____

How many points do you have left
from today?   + _____

Number of points in the bank: + _____
                                                     _____

                                         Total   _____

BANK TIME!

You can now spend points, or Bank them for use
later. That way you can save up for bigger
prizes!

                    Total from above   _____

        Cost of prize, if you picked one - _____
                                             _____

    Total left to go back to the bank   _____

Go now to page 113. BE SURE TO RECORD YOUR
TOTAL IN THE BANK. Save up your points--
you'll be able spend them at a later time.

SESSION 17: YOU'RE THE EXPERT

Hello, again! Before we get started today, go over your STIC task from last week. Discuss your solutions with your therapist, and if you did a good job, give yourself the bonus points!

You and your therapist have been creating problem situations, talking over and acting out the possible ways to react in these situations, and deciding on the best way to respond in these situations. We will be continuing to do this for the next few sessions, as well. By the time you reach Session 20, you will be the expert!

As the expert, you can select a situation that you feel best presents the steps of problem solving. And, as the expert, you can tell about it to someone else. That is, we will work together to make a commercial in which you are the star. A commercial about how to be a good problem solver.

Start to think about a commercial in which you show other people how to STOP AND THINK. It could be a poem, or a rap song, or anything else you want to try. Just like the problem solving we did for many weeks now, we can problem-solve the type of commercial to produce.

You could create your own cartoon character, if you like, and draw a comic strip that illustrates your cartoon character thinking about solving a problem. Or your presentation could be like a radio, TV, or newspaper ad. Part of today's work will be fun--to talk about and think of ideas for your own commercial! Take 15 minutes and, along with your therapist, think about ideas for your commercial.

After 15 minutes, turn the page over and continue.

Now that you have had a chance to come up with lots
of ideas, and maybe even select the one that you
want to do, take the next 10 or 15 minutes and make
plans. If you haven't yet chosen one idea, make your
selection now. Write it down in the space below.

_____

_____

Now that you have an idea, we still need to think
about materials, props, equipment.

What equipment will be needed?

Will a script be needed?

Who will act in the commercial?

What props would be useful?

If it is a print commercial, will you use color?

Be sure to tape record your commercial, so others
can actually get to hear it.

If you want to make a videotape, do you have access
to the needed equipment?

Take the next 15 minutes and start to work on your
commercial. Your therapist is there to help, so
feel free to ask for input and try out your ideas.
Together, I bet you'll do a terrific job. In fact,
I very much want to see what you produce. If you
can, make a copy for me, Detective Dan, and send it
to me at my home address, 238 Meeting House Lane,
Merion Station, PA 19066 USA (see the form on page
125). I will be sure to acknowledge your work.

YOUR STIC TASK FOR NEXT TIME:

Think more about your idea for a commercial. What
materials might work better than others? Write down
any questions that you might have...we will talk
about them next session.
When you meet your therapist next time you can earn
points by discussing your plans for the commercial.

See you next time!

HOW DID YOU DO TODAY?

Your rating:	1	2	3	4	5
	Not So Hot	O.K.	Good	Very Good	Super
Therapist's rating:	1	2	3	4	5

Do the ratings agree (within 1 point)?
If they do, you get 2 points!   + _____

Did you remember to do your STIC task?
If you did you get 2 points!   + _____

How many points do you have left
from today?   + _____

Number of points in the bank: + _____
                                                     _____

                                        Total   _____

```
+--------------------------------------------------+
|                   BANK TIME!                     |
|                                                  |
|  You can now spend points, or Bank them for use  |
|  later. That way you can save up for bigger      |
|  prizes!                                         |
|                                                  |
|                Total from above      _____     |
|                                                  |
|    Cost of prize, if you picked one  - _____   |
|                                       _____    |
|                                                  |
|    Total left to go back to the bank  _____    |
|                                                  |
|                                                  |
|  Go now to page 113.  BE SURE TO RECORD YOUR     |
|  TOTAL IN THE BANK.  Save up your points--       |
|  you'll be able spend them at a later time.      |
+--------------------------------------------------+
```

SESSION 18: LET'S REVIEW

Hi, there! Did you remember to think about your commercial? Go over the idea with your therapist...you might get to award yourself a 2-point bonus!

So far you have learned a lot of different ways to think about and react to problem situations. Good work! Today we are going to review the problem-solving steps you have learned. I'll bet you know them by heart. Take out your "STOP AND THINK" stop sign and give it to your therapist. Now, from memory, go through the steps.

Great!

Remember that Session 20 will be for making your commercial. This is your chance to teach someone else how to solve problems. We'll take today to review the steps one at a time using some new situations. Think of some situations that are really difficult for you. Ask your therapist, too. Working together, make a list of your three toughest problems. Then, think through some of the possible solutions.

Use your own problems. If you want to use one of our suggestions, you can. There are several on the next page.

1. You are playing a game of tennis. You think your serve was in-bounds, but your opponent claims that it went out. How do you react?

2. You call and invite a friend to come over after school. Ten minutes later another friend of yours calls and invites you to a special event. You have just made plans with your other friend, so you can't say yes. What can you do?

3. You see three older kids hitting a smaller, younger child. No one else sees this except you. What might you do?

4. You agree to trade to a friend something of yours that is special to you--in return you will get something of theirs. Later that day you think about it again and you wish that you hadn't agreed to the trade. What would you do?

5. Your grandparent calls and asks whether you like the birthday present sent to you. For this problem, we will pretend that you **don't** like it! What do you say?

It's best if you use your own situations today. Create your own situation and write it down in the space provided.

_____

_____

_____

Now we'll use the steps to solve the problem. Say the steps out loud as you do them.

WHAT DO YOU DO FIRST?

WHAT COMES SECOND?

WHAT IS THE THIRD STEP?

WHAT NEXT?

ANYTHING ELSE?

GOOD JOB! You are ready to teach these skills to someone else! Before we move on, however, let's solve one more case.

Write down a situation that you and your therapist agree can be a problem situation for you.

_____

_____

_____

WHAT DO YOU DO FIRST?

WHAT COMES SECOND?

AND THEN?

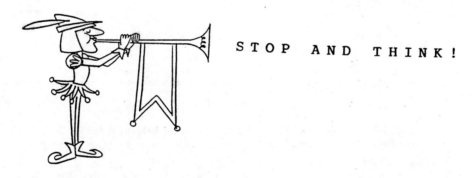 S T O P   A N D   T H I N K !

YOUR STIC TASK FOR NEXT TIME:
Sometime before next session, there is likely to be a problem...even if it's a small one. Your STIC task is to identify a problem that involved you and another person. When we meet next time, you will describe the problem, the possible ways to resolve the problem, and also what actually happened.

Also, next week is dress rehearsal for your commercial. Be prepared to try out your ideas for practice.

Keep up the good work!

Until next time...

HOW DID YOU DO TODAY?

Your rating:	1	2	3	4	5
	Not So Hot	O.K.	Good	Very Good	Super
Therapist's rating:	1	2	3	4	5

Do the ratings agree (within 1 point)?
If they do, you get 2 points!   + _____

Did you remember to do your STIC task?
If you did you get 2 points!   + _____

How many points do you have left
from today?   + _____

Number of points in the bank: + _____
                                                  _____
                                    Total   _____

```
+-----------------------------------------------------+
|                     BANK TIME!                      |
|                                                     |
|  You can now spend points, or Bank them for use     |
|  later. That way you can save up for bigger         |
|  prizes!                                            |
|                                                     |
|               Total from above      _____         |
|                                                     |
|      Cost of prize, if you picked one   - _____   |
|                                      _____  |
|                                                     |
|  Total left to go back to the bank   _____        |
|                                                     |
|                                                     |
|  Go now to page 113.  BE SURE TO RECORD YOUR        |
|  TOTAL IN THE BANK.  Save up your points--          |
|  you'll be able spend them at a later time.         |
+-----------------------------------------------------+
```

BE PROUD OF YOURSELF!

SESSION 19: DRESS REHEARSAL

Before we get started today, let's take a few minutes to go over your STIC task with your therapist. Go ahead and take several minutes. By the way, it's OK to brag to your therapist about being a good problem solver. Be proud of your efforts!

We only have two meetings left, so now is a good time for us to think more about your final project for next session--the commercial.

You are the star...YOU become the teacher!

By the way, if you come up with some good ideas, don't be shy about it! Send them to Detective Dan (see page 125). If you would like, and I would have to have your permission, I'll be sure to include your first name and your ideas in the next edition of the Stop and Think Workbook.

YOUR STIC TASK FOR NEXT TIME

Do you have all the materials that you will need for your commercial? If there are any materials that you will need, and you haven't brought them in yet, make a list now. Also, decide when you will check your list and gather all of your materials. The STIC task is to bring in any and all materials that you will need.

HOW DID YOU DO TODAY?

Your rating:	1	2	3	4	5
	Not So Hot	O.K.	Good	Very Good	Super
Therapist's rating:	1	2	3	4	5

Do the ratings agree (within 1 point)?
If they do, you get 2 points!   + _____

Did you remember to do your STIC task?
If you did you get 2 points!   + _____

How many points do you have left
from today?   + _____

Number of points in the bank: + _____
                                                     _____

                                      Total   _____

BANK TIME!

You can now spend points, or Bank them for use later. That way you can save up for bigger prizes!

              Total from above   _____

   Cost of prize, if you picked one   - _____
                                         _____

Total left to go back to the bank   _____

Go now to page 113. BE SURE TO RECORD YOUR TOTAL IN THE BANK. Save up your points-- you'll be able spend them at a later time.

SESSION 20: YOU MADE IT !!!

Today will be the most fun session of all. You have learned a lot in the time we have worked together. You have become a good problem-solving detective. As Detective Dan knows...

Identify the problem
Think of a few choices
Think of how you and others will feel
Make a plan and try it out!
Reward yourself.

You've put the steps in your own words, and that is how it should be...but I bet Dan's words are familiar to you!

You have learned how to solve all kinds of problems using your steps. You can continue to use these steps to solve any problem that comes your way. Congratulations!

Today you are the star. Depending on what you chose to do for your commercial, you get to show your therapist your work. Was it a print commercial? A song? A poster? A comic strip? Have a good time sharing your special project with your therapist. Be sure to tape it...and remember that, if you have an extra copy, Detective Dan would love to see your work.

Don't forget to cash in your points and enjoy your rewards! You have earned them!

You are now ready to receive the certificate at the end of this workbook. Your therapist will fill out the information and sign it for you.

CONGRATULATIONS! YOU HAVE A RIGHT TO BE VERY PROUD OF YOURSELF!!!

```
┌─────────────────────────────────────────────┐
│ ::::::::::::::::::::::::::::::::::::::::::::::: │
│                                               │
│        M Y   R E W A R D   S H O P            │
│                                               │
│ ::::::::::::::::::::::::::::::::::::::::::::::: │
└─────────────────────────────────────────────┘
```

Here is your chance to create
just the kind of store you would
like to shop in. Take some time
now to discuss with your therapist
the kinds of items you would like
to have available to you--items
that you can purchase with the
Stop and Think dollars (points)
that you will earn from your
workbook sessions. Your therapist can help guide you
in suggesting some items for your Reward Shop, and
will help in deciding how many points you will have to
pay to purchase each of these items. No televisions
or trips to Hawaii: try to think of inexpensive items
that would be of interest to you.

After you have discussed your Reward Shop items
with your therapist, make a list of them below. Be
sure to record how many points will be required to
purchase each item.

ITEMS THAT I MAY PURCHASE: PRICE:

1._____   ___ points

2._____   ___ points

3._____   ___ points

4._____   ___ points

5._____   ___ points

6._____   ___ points

7.___color marker_____   ___ points

8.___snack_____   ___ points

111

THE BANK

RECORD THE POINTS YOU HAVE LEFT FROM EACH SESSION
KEEP A RUNNING TOTAL IN THE SPACES BELOW:

SESS 1	SESS 2	SESS 3	SESS 4	SESS 5

SESS 6	SESS 7	SESS 8	SESS 9	SESS 10

SESS 11	SESS 12	SESS 13	SESS 14	SESS 15

SESS 16	SESS 17	SESS 18	SESS 19	SESS 20

CUT   THIS   OUT

115

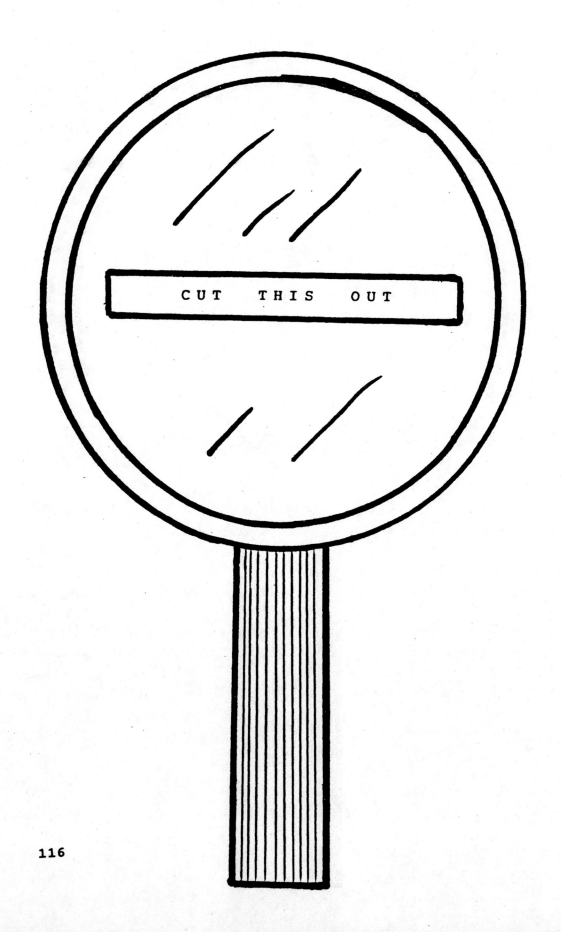

CUT THIS OUT

STOP & THINK

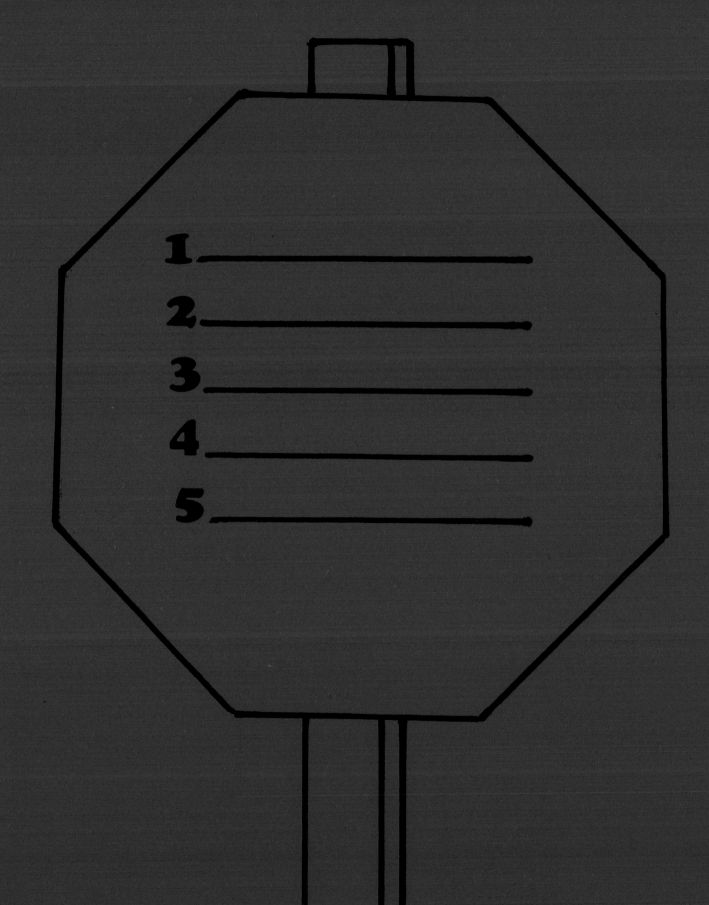

1. _____

2. _____

3. _____

4. _____

5. _____

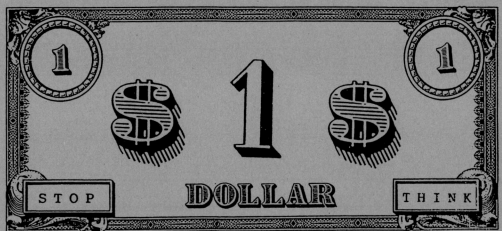

119

SITUATION CARDS

You finished your work and now you have nothing to do.	The kid next to you begins to tease you.
You are talking to a group and someone interrupts you.	Someone bumps into you by accident.
Some kids are playing a game and you want to join in.	You and some other kids want to play different games.
Your mom/dad has asked you to help with some work around the house, and a friend comes to ask you to play.	After school you have homework to do, a favorite TV program to watch, and a friend asks you to play.
You are working on an assignment and you come across a problem that you can't solve.	You are in school and working quietly, but a friend tries to get you to fool around.
You and a brother or sister are fighting over a game.	On the playground, a child tries to start a fight with you.
In a group, you offer an idea, but no one seems to like it.	The teacher asks a question and you do not know the answer.
You are listening to someone talk, and he says something that you know is wrong.	Someone took something from your desk, and you think you know who did it.

BLANK SITUATION CARDS

WHAT DO YOU THINK?

Your Name: _____ Age: _____
(You may use your first name only, if you wish.)

Your Address: _____

_____ ZIP _____

Your therapist's name: _____

So tell me, what do you think? Use extra sheets as needed.

Detective Dan has been very impressed with the ideas that children have shared with him and he might want to mention **your** ideas to other children. If he does, he will mention your name. Will you give him your permission? Please complete the following.

I, _____, give Detective Dan
       (your name)
permission to mention my ideas to other children,

as in a future edition of the Stop and Think

Workbook. _____
                  (sign your name here)

FROM: _____
      _____
      _____

```
                                         ┌──────────────┐
                                         │              │
                                         │    Stamp     │
                                         │              │
                                         └──────────────┘
```

┌───┐
│ TO: Detective Dan   │
│   208 Llanfair Road   │
│   Ardmore, PA   19003   │
│   U S A   │
└───┘